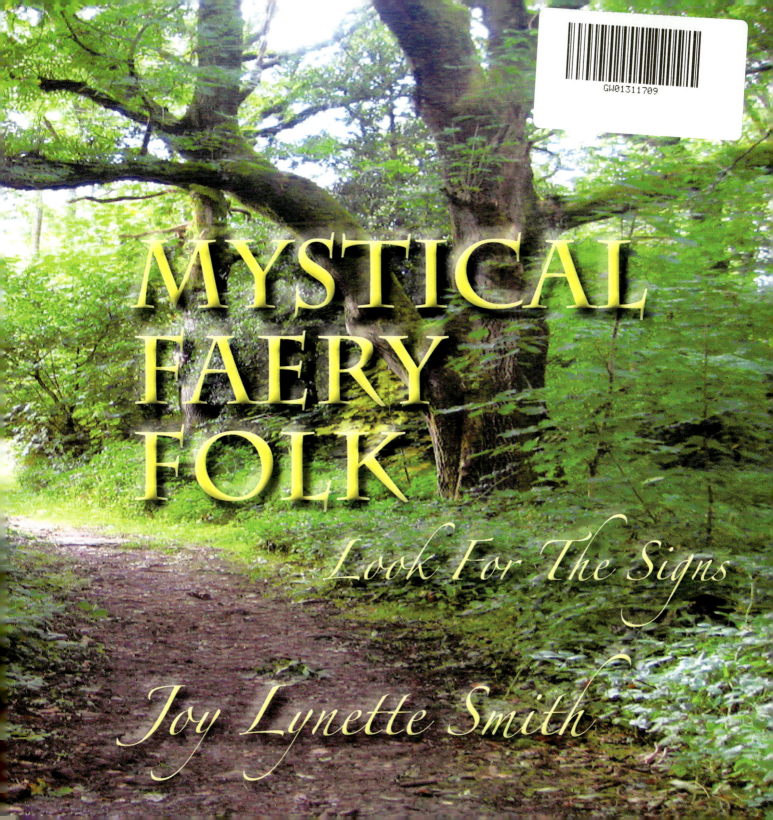

AuthorHouse™
1663 Liberty Drive
Bloomington, IN 47403
www.authorhouse.com
Phone: 1-800-839-8640

© 2013 Joy Lynette Smith. All Rights Reserved.

Graphic Designer: Mervyn J. A. Smith

No part of this book may be reproduced, stored in a retrieval system,
or transmitted by any means without the written permission of the author.

Published by AuthorHouse 12/27/2012

ISBN: 978-1-4772-4228-5 (sc)
        978-1-4772-4229-2 (e)

Library of Congress Control Number: 2012920352

All images used in this book are the property of Mervyn J. A. & Joy Lynette Smith. Any person
depicted has given permission for their image to be used in the book.

This book is printed on acid-free paper.

Because of the dynamic nature of the Internet, any web addresses or links contained in this book may have changed
since publication and may no longer be valid. The views expressed in this work are solely those of the author and do not
necessarily reflect the views of the publisher, and the publisher hereby disclaims any responsibility for them.

Dedication

Luke Harken – exuberant, curious, joyful • Dedication: This book is dedicated to my absolutely delightful grandchildren Justin, Holly and

Foreword

So many laugh or roll their eyes on hearing one claim to see a fairy. Reactions are more so if one claims to communicate with the Devic Realms and Fairy Kingdoms. Some express dismay that this is not to be an aspect of their path in this lifetime. Others, sadly, merely pretend that this is their reality as well, to be able commune with parallel kingdoms and universes.

It has been my blessing for as long as I can remember to actually see, communicate and literally work with those on the Devic Realms.

Great wisdom has been imparted to me by the little folk and tree devas I have happened upon in the Australian bush and European forest, woodlands and gardens. Their roles in maintaining and tending forests and gardens is so involved and through me these ones have been able to give some advice they would like to be shared with mankind.

In Grizedale Forest in the glorious English Lake District there is an area where non-native trees have been planted in very damp soil, so that the roots are always saturated. As with many forests of trees grown for commercial purposes there is little or no plant layering or infrastructure between these conifers. The little folk and tree devas can be stymied by such plantings. In a natural woodland many plants, ferns and shrubs grow in harmony and abundance among the trees. These ones are guided by our thoughts in determining their actions.

If we are to spend our energies on thinking about the problems we have presented to them this will not be productive. The advice I have been given is to focus on what is growing well, to visualise what has been done correctly and hold that vision. This way those on the Devic Realms are best able to produce healthy plants, exactly as set in the seed or seedling, no matter where we have chosen to place them.

Flowers grow brighter, more vibrantly and there tend to be many more blossoms when one takes time to acknowledge the efforts of the Devic Realms. The foliage will also appear so glossy and smooth, as if it had been polished – and it usually is!

Sometimes an individual tree is the guardian of a sacred site, a gate-keeper, if you like. By walking slowly and silently, through woodlands and being alert and watchful such icons can become visible to all. Suddenly one tree may shimmer and radiate light or its leaves may shine more than others of the same type growing nearby.

If children feel sad that they are not yet able to see Fairy Folk it is helpful to encourage them to keep trying. While they are focussed on the Fairy Kingdom children can become more aware of how best to treat the Mother Earth and all that is on her surface.

When young ones claim that they are seeing fairies – believe them as they most likely are!

Joy Lynette Smith, September 2012

Contents

Faery Kettle	4	*Holly Grove*	54
The Faery Kirk	6	*Wellow Faeries*	56
Faery Bridge	8	*Giant Bamboo Kalamunda*	58
Underwood	10	*Blue Delphinium Faeries*	60
Yew Tree	12	*Holy Well St Barbe*	62
Yew Tree Faery	14	*Pine Tree near Hotié De Viviane*	64
Faery Steps	16	*Forest around Castel Franc*	66
Underwood Faery	18	*Vortex Castel Franc*	68
Sea Wood	20	*Sainte Julianne*	70
Sea Wood Little Man	22	*La Magdalene Yoni Stone*	72
Grizedale Forest	24	*La Magdalene Ancient Cave*	74
Grizedale Forest Little Man	26	*Well South of St Barbe*	76
Cherry Tree Faery	28	*River Gum*	78
St Madron's Well	30	*Violet Faeries*	80
St Nectan's Glen	32	*Water Faeries - Mount Pleasant*	82
Forest near Trebetherick	34	*Indian Coral Tree*	84
Brown Willy	36	*Tingle Forest*	86
Isabella Plantation	38	*Grandma Tingle*	88
Cedar Tree Kew Gardens	40	*Snowy Mountain Gum*	90
Red Geranium Faery	42	*Wattle Faeries*	92
Three Trees Common	44	*Silk Cotton Tree*	94
Mother Tree	46	*The Poplar Tree*	96
Giant Willow – Faery Kingdom	48	*Our Faraway Tree*	98
Cymbidium Faery	50	*Holly's Faery Garden*	100
Faeries West Kennet Long Barrow	52	*Camphor Laurel Tree*	102

Faery Kettle

Sound calls one from afar
Water roaring
Path through forest past the mill
Water roaring louder still

Meandering path beside gushing stream
Spring abounds in glorious green
Gradually turns and rises to where
One can merely stand and stare

Faery Kettle waterfall
Sounds abound kettle catches all
Water swirling round and round
Over the edge and falling down

Water rolling at a pace
Overflowing gracefully at this place
Silken water flowing down
Faery Folk surround in grace

Faery Kettle

Water rolling at a pace, Overflowing gracefully at a place, Silken water flowing down, Faery Folk surround in grace.

The Faery Kirk

Climb over fence and slide down path
Keep Faery Kettle on your left
Turn to your right and enter there
Go right into the dim dark cleft

For this is a truly sacred site
For each and every Faery
They visit here come day, come night
As this is the Faery's Kirk

Light seems to glow from within
And beckons all Faery Folk in
The Kirk is where they come to bless
To offer love and thankfulness

If ever you come upon this sacred place
Doff your hat, wear a smile on your face
Do not linger but go off at a pace
For the Faery Kirk is for their race

A Faery Kirk such as this
Entered through cleft in stone wall
Is not for such as me and you
In respect of all that Faery Folk do

The Faery Kirk

As this is the Faery's Kirk • For this is a truly sacred site, For each and every Faery, They visit here come day come night,

Faery Bridge

Magically stretching across the stream
Silken waters all agleam
Sliding over green mossy rocks
Gleaming grasses and old fallen logs

For those who are blessed with 'Second Sight'
This tiny bridge makes the heart feel light
Flying all about with tinkling sound
Faery Folk are to be found

Birches glistening, leaves so bright
Tended with love as is their right
Water drops below this place
To Faery Kettle in all its grace

Faery Folk are in this stream
Helping keep these waters clean
Within the sounds – Shhh! Not a word!
Their tinkling laughter can be heard

Emerald moss aglow upon the rocks on each shore
Faery Folk tend to these and so much more
Every flower, leaf and stone
Not one is left to grow alone

Faery Bridge which spans the stream
Where everything that lives does gleam
A place to thank the Faery Folk
For everything is not as it seems

Faery Bridge

Faery Folk are to be found • For those who are blessed with 'Second Sight' This tiny bridge makes the heart feel light Playing all about with tinkling sound

Underwood

Enter the forest in a well-mannered way
The Little Folk will hear you pray
They'll follow your journey from side of path
Catch their eye – they'll make you laugh!

For they've lived in this place for many a year
Actually as long as the Underwood
Their homes can be seen here
In mossy rock, tree and fallen wood

They walk beside you all the way
To the little Yew
Observing every step you take
Mimicking you!

This forest is so light by day
The Little Folk prefer to play
To visit here in darkest night
Would be a very different plight.

Underwood

Enter the forest in a well-mannered way · The Little Folk will hear you pray · They'll follow your journey from side of path · Catch their eye – they'll make you laugh!

Yew Tree

About the end of Underwood
This little tree of Yew is stood
The guardian of Faery Steps
Shining emerald upon it seen
Are Faery Folk clothed in red and green

Their task to keep this tree
Obvious to those who see
Polishing leaves till they glisten
The Faeries' job is to listen
For those who ask for permission

A glowing green orb is sent to earth
To passers-by who've asked the right
This shines on the path to the right
And the petite Yew shines with all its might

Yew Tree

About the end of Underwood · This little tree of Yew is stood · The guardian of Faery Steps · Shining emerald upon it seen · Faery Folk clothed in red and green ·

Yew Tree Faery

So small he looked upon the Yew tree
I heard him as he called to me
'If you'd step up as I have planned
I'll come and sit upon your hand'

So pleased was I when he spoke to me
That I followed his advice explicitly
Then down upon my hand he came
Stretched up to my ear and whispered his name

To share such truth was such a surprise
Tears welled and flowed from both my eyes
A faery's name is so sacred
'Twas a blessing to be so honoured

One day upon his tree I came
The little one who'd shared his name
A gentle giant of a man with me did walk
About this Yew Faery we did talk

To the Yew Faery I did plead
To climb on my hand and he agreed
Then he stepped onto the man's huge hand
And sat there looking so proud and grand

His auric field the man could feel
And realised this one was real
The tiny faery's heart sent such love
From one so small was more than enough

So compassionately did the man turn to me
Then I placed the Yew Faery back upon his tree
'Bless you and thank you Yew Tree Faery'

Yew Tree Faery

So small he looked upon Yew Tree I heard him, he called to me, 'If you'd step up as I planned I'll come and sit upon your hand'

Faery Steps

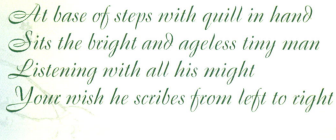

At base of steps with quill in hand
Sits the bright and ageless tiny man
Listening with all his might
Your wish he scribes from left to right

As upon the steps you tread
He observes and shakes his head
Another sits above the stairs
With sparkling eyes he also glares

His quill he holds ready to write
As above the steps he sits astride
Legs crossed, huge book on knee
He observes your upwards glide

If either sees you touch the face
Of rock that holds these steps in place
A frown will come upon their face
Your wish a struck line will erase

So carefully climb with measured stride
Never touching either side
Then you will be filled with great bliss
As Faery Folk grant your Wish

Faery Steps

As Faery Folk grant your Wish • So carefully climb with measured stride • Never touching either side • Then you will be filled with great bliss

Underwood Faery

Pause at the stone pillars
And make a silent prayer
Before entering Underwood
Be well-mannered – understood?

Then enter slowly, open your eyes
Who knows, you may have a surprise
Those who live in Underwood
Know you've behaved as you should

Once on a stroll through these ancient woods
With a friend certainly who understood
I pointed out a very odd sight
All was still but up to our right

One leaf was waving of its own accord
In all directions, quite absurd
All else was still, Underwood was quiet
She saw this leaf move, it caused her some disquiet

For I could see the tiny faery ringing
Holding the leaf like it was a church bell
Ringing and laughing and singing
So infectious that we both laughed as well

My friend now knows that if you ask permission
Before you enter Underwood
And then expect nothing but be open
Most wonderful things can happen

Underwood Faery

Then enter slowly, open your eyes · Who knows, you may have a surprise · Those who live in Underwood · Know you've behaved as you should ·

Sea Wood

Tinkling laughter, so many smiles
Arms and shoulders clothed in faeries
Eyes awash with tears of merriment
Memories of great sentiment

In this old forest some have seen
Little Folk dressed in brown and green
They've stood in front and doffed their hat
Turned and left and that was that

Others have met tiny Faery Folk
Moving past all a flutter by
Tending flowers, tidying leaves
Thinking first 'That's a butterfly!'

More have sat in silence
And met a Tree Deva in its magnificence
Their lives have been forever changed
After such moments of pure innocence

What a wondrous place is this
That's brought so many to such bliss.

Sea Wood

Tinkling laughter so many smiles Arms and shoulders clothed in faeries Eyes anash with tears of merriment Memories of great sentiment

Sea Wood Little Man

Walking softly, lost in my own thoughts
Through Sea Wood one balmy summer day
I noticed a slight movement just over the way
I blinked and then I blinked once more

Rubbed my eyes and my, oh my
There sat a little man, a tiny little guy
Clothed in green jacket and brown trousers
A floppy at the top red hat

Brown boots with turned over tops
All made of sturdy fabrics
His beard was long and snowy white
Moustache so huge both left and right

He doffed his hat and greeted me
'Welcome fair lady to this wood'
Surprised when he spoke I responded
With a 'Thank you, kind Sir' as one should

Another flash of movement then
I blinked and then I blinked again
There was no sign of the little man
Though I looked as hard as I can

What a blessing to receive such a greeting
And to meet this tiny guy
Though it was only fleeting
Has left me feeling high

Now when I walk through Sea Wood
I know there's more here than meets the eye
And think perhaps this time I may see
The little man who once greeted me

Sea Wood Little Man

A floppy at the top red hat • Rubbed my eyes and my, oh my, There sat a little man, a tiny little guy Dressed in green jacket and brown trousers

Grizedale Forest

Man-made forest what a tale
Two little men of Grizedale
Plead with me to always bring
Memory to the shining things

'Our plight is tough
The soil is shallow
There's not soil enough
Tree roots do wallow'

Standing each on shining mossy stone
They beg 'Don't let us do this task alone'
Clothed in red, green and brown
Nuggety faces all afrown

'Our task is grim' they say to me
'Please listen to our earnest plea.
Man's ignorance does make us forlorn
But with your aid this can be borne.'

Our help is needed with their task
This is all of us they ask:
'When the image of Grizedale your mind brings
Please remember the shining things.'

Grizedale Forest

'Our plight is tough The soil is shallow There's not soil enough Tree roots go shallow,' They beg, 'Don't let us do this task alone!'

25

Grizedale Forest Little Man

We once came to visit Grizedale Forest
And were shocked to find a huge area denuded
Upon our senses this intruded
So we held a healing service

We sent love and compassion
To all the stunned and mourning tree devas
Whose trees had so brutally gone

We turned and walked through the pines
Tall, majestic reaching ever upwards
A stunningly beautiful
Natural cathedral

This area was still, silent
Like everything was holding its breath, listening
A place of potent power
Huge trunks with specks of sunlight glistening

Quietly we parted, each to contemplate
To listen and observe the peacefulness of this place

Then back to the cathedral we returned
One by one, our minds all churned
For each had a shared experience unknowingly
One by one we told the same story

Each of us had seen, not only one or two
A little fellow walking by dressed in blue and green
A hooded cape of darkest blue
Covering his face so it couldn't be seen

Amazed were we to have all seen
This tiny man clothed in blue and green
Surprised, honoured and blessed were we
To share such a precious memory

Grizedale Forest Little Man

Huge trunks with specks of sunlight glistening • This area was still, silent • Like everything was holding its breath, listening • A place of potent power

Cherry Tree Faery

Strolling through this London Park
Stunning cherry trees all a-bloom, pale and dark
Either side of one
Covered in delicate flowers,
Lovely in the sun

My goodness me
What is this I see
On the delightful rose pink cherry tree?
The Cherry Tree Faery

Clothed in frothy skirt of rosy pink down
The Cherry Tree Faery gently flutters down
Upon her head a hat to match
To her elegant style mine's not a patch

Her feet are clothed in vibrant green
An emerald purse on wrist is seen
Layers of pink so vibrant and bright
Beauteous creature in her own right

Cherry Tree Faery

My goodness me What is this I see On the delightful rose pink cherry tree? It's The Cherry Tree Faery •

St Madron's Well

Leave the path and go through the trees
They are welcoming and have been here for an age
Weave in and out, keep your head down
This is a place of healing and pilgrimage

First the stone pillars, the steps and then the tree
It is truly covered with many a cloutie
Many others have come here to pray
To wash all their problems away

Back to the path then turn to the left
St Madron's Well is in the cleft
The water flows through old stone wall
This Chapel has no roof at all

This is a place of sanctuary
With clear, fresh, vibrant water flowing
Many visit here annually
A place of gentle knowing

Back along the path I saw
So many faeries, by the score
Back at the cloutie tree
There were many, many more

I asked of them their role with the clouties
They answered me most joyfully
'We listen carefully and read all requests
And if they've been asked selflessly
Then do all we can to make them happen
According to the laws that are given karmically'

So when the cloth tied to the tree
Falls to the ground to meld with the Earth anew
Then the prayer has been answered truthfully
And your wish has been granted too

St Madron's Well

A place of gentle knowing • Back along the path I saw So many faeries, by the score Back at the cloutie tree There were even more

St Nectan's Glen

Wandering through the woods
Along the edge of the river
'Tis wonderful indeed
It truly makes one quiver

This is a place of wonderment
It's truly seeped in amazing history
For along these paths in medieval times
Even rode the crusaders before their journey

In tiny caves and under little water-falls
The Faery Folk reside
They watch us pass, come one come all
As they stand on either side

For centuries they have seen us pass
Strolling down to the Kieve and Waterfall
Their memories hold it all
The local history

The Faery Folk have recorded all along
The people who've gone by
Monks and maidens, knights on horseback
Mothers with new babies, the frail, the strong

The Faery Folk have listened to the reasons
That people have travelled, whatever the seasons
For they are guardians of the entry
To this ancient way

St Nectan's Glen

This local history • For centuries they have seen us pass Strolling down to the Kieve and Waterfall Their memories record it all

Forest near Trebetherick

First go to the church at St Enodoc
Its steeple is all awry
Last place of Sir John Betjeman
A truly amazing guy

Walk around the meadows and
Head away from the beach
Find a little forest there
It's not difficult to reach

Enter this forest and stand quite still
Be calm and breath quietly
Then open you eyes very slowly
Look to the side, if you will

For this tiny area is so magical
Faeries sit upon rocks
Their laughter quite infectious
Do look carefully, it's like they are there in flocks!

I first went there in November
Twas a cold but fine day
But in the forest it felt warm
To be among the fey

Forest near Trebetherick

I first went there in November
'Twas a cold but fine day
But in the forest it felt warm
To be among the fey
There in flocks

Brown Willy

Walk up Rough Tor and over the ridge
Down the other side and on again
To the very bottom where there's a fence
Step up and up and climb on over

Through corner of eye upon the ground
A tiny little fellow I found
Doff of his hat and off he bounds
Happy to go a roving

Just a glimpse of this cheery fellow
Hat of brown, trousers too
His coat of deepest yellow
His crinkled eyes were clearest blue

His beard was long and white as snow
It seemed that it would grow and grow
Moustaches grew so long on both sides
Surely were a work of pride

Twas only a glimpse I saw of him
He seemed to be there and then quite dim
Although I could no longer see this one
I felt him beside me as I climbed the mountain

For the plan was to climb Brown Willy
Quite an effort but never silly
Feeling this tiny fellow by my side
I took the climb within my stride

Brown Willy

Just a glimpse of this cheery fellow · Hat of brown, trousers too · His coat of deepest yellow · His crinkled eyes were clearest blue

Isabella Plantation

Awash with colour, our senses alive
In gardens like this, do faeries thrive

Beneath ancient oaks
Rainbows of glorious colour
Azaleas, Rhododendrons, Camellias
In all their splendour
The Faery Folk have these to tender

This stunningly beautiful plantation
Is home for so many Faery Folk
They toil without expectation
For them this is never like a yoke

People flock here each and every season
To embrace this stunning beauty is their reason

Streams are clad in greens of many hues
Bluebells ringing with deepest blues
Ferns uncurling their Fibonacci spirals
Glorious, such absolute perfection,
Draws us in each and every direction

Perfumes exquisite, senses alive
It's here that Faery Folk do thrive

Isabella Plantation

It's here that Faery Folk do thrive • Glorious, such absolute perfection Trans us in each and every direction Perfumes exquisite, senses alive

Cedar Tree Kew Gardens

Standing proudly near top of hill
To see this Cedar is such a thrill
Branches spread out so wide
Magnificence – Oh, how I sighed!

Below Cedar upon the ground
The Cedar Roses can be found
Fibonacci Spirals of perfection
Coming out in a single direction

From the Cedar Roses had fallen seeds
The Earth looked after all their needs
So on the ground midst ivy spread
Baby Cedars raised their heads

Behind Cedar and under his cover
There are many Cedars – one after the other
Crowding around one so wise
Respect and honour in their eyes

Cedar spoke with a deep but soft voice
I heard his words but barely any noise
He felt Kew Gardens were a Cedar haven
The gardeners to had him so much care given

He told me to open my eyes
Look around me and see that truthfully
How many of his family could thrive
And live here most comfortably

Cedar Tree Kew Gardens

Coming out in one direction • Below Cedar upon the ground The Cedar Roses can be found Fibonacci Spirals of perfection

Red Geranium Faery

Outside kitchen in window box
Were red geranium flowers
The most beautiful fairy tended them
Right at this home of ours

Red Geranium Faery
Takes her work most seriously
Carefully tending each bud, leaf and flower
Dainty hands working industriously

Pretty faery wears a red hat
A single geranium flower
Her dress is deepest scarlet
Layers of red petals around her

The Geranium flowers
In all their splendour
Grow within hours
It is indeed a wonder

Now we have our plants inside
The lovely faery takes great pride
Moving around most gracefully
Bringing so much joy for all to see

Red Geranium Faery

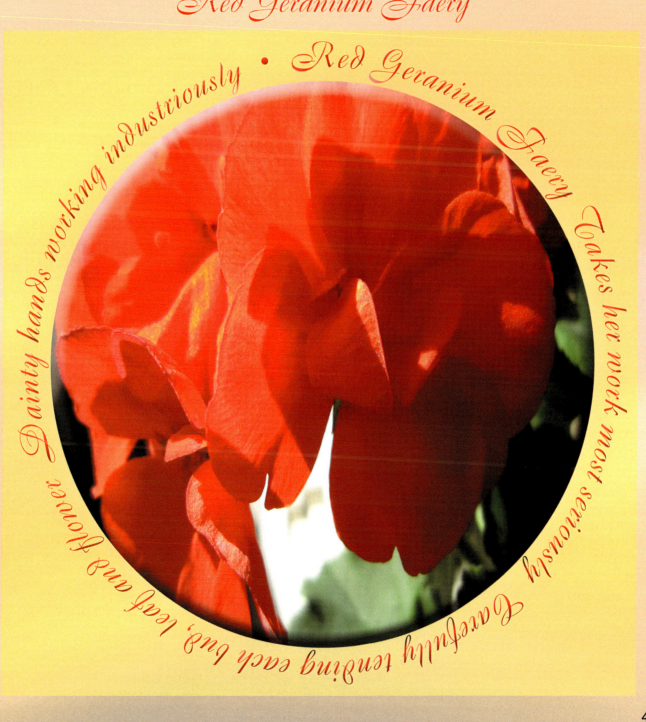

Red Geranium Faery takes her work most seriously Carefully tending each bud, leaf and flower Dainty hands working industriously

Three Trees Common

Branches spread wide, heads together
Three Trees Common work forever
Beautiful to behold indeed
Clothed in greens of every shade

Sadly one tree has been pollarded
Its sisters, tested, work much harder
Protecting her through the seasons
They work together for their reasons

Three Trees Common forgive the action
Though it brought man such satisfaction
They know he worked in ignorance
'Bless and bring wisdom' is their stance

To stand within their silent space
All noise of London will erase
A place of serenity they have created
Peaceful beauty not abated

Stand in their dappled light
Three Trees Common have such insight
Clear you minds as there you stand
Let in their thoughts – they understand

Your problems to them are not new
They've listened to so many before you
For truly they are so wise
Three Trees Common

Three Trees Common

Clothed in greens of every shade • Branches spread wide, heads together Three Trees Common mark forever Beautiful to behold indeed

Mother Tree

On Wandsworth Common is the Mother Tree
Standing so magnificently
Ancient, wise one, glorious to see

For those who stop and study her base
They'll see great twisted strands in place
For this giant stands where ley lines cross
At the edge of Wandsworth Common

Each year she is the last to drop her leaves
Later than most people would believe
She's still in leaf when all others are bare
All across Wandsworth Common

Then so soon every year we see
Leaf buds on this lovely tree
Every other tree is still asleep
All across Wandsworth Common

In no time at all she's covered in leaf
Then glorious pyramidal candles – Good grief!
Every other tree is still asleep
All around Wandsworth Common

The Wisdom Keeper is this but
No ordinary everyday Horse Chestnut
For every tree learns from her
All over Wandsworth Common

She's seen so much over all her years
Her knowledge can allay your fears
Using ley lines her thoughts to share
Emanating from Wandsworth Common

Mother Tree

On Wandsworth Common is the Mother Tree
Standing oh so magnificently
Ancient, wise one, glorious to see

Giant Willow – Faery Kingdom

Gnarled trunk by edge of pond
Years ago I happened upon
Distracted by strange noise and movement
Towards the tree, over the fence, I bent

Massive trunks spread wide in all directions
Above and below in the water's reflections
Confused I listened for a sound
And noticed Faery Folk all around

Their homes, I saw, were in this tree
Generations living there peacefully
Young and old on this Willow resided
For many years it had their home provided

So blessed I felt to see this place
That I left them there with humble grace

Every time I wander by this Willow
Be it in winter, spring, summer or autumn
The Faery Folk always bid me welcome
Now that they know that I have come

Some wave, some laugh, some bow
Their welcome is tangible anyhow
Long leaves protect, gnarled bark home for some
The King George's Willow is truly a Faery Kingdom

Giant Willow - Faery Kingdom

Gnarled trunk by edge of pond Some years ago I happened upon Distracted by strange noise and movement Towards the tree, over the fence, I bent

Cymbidium Faery

Polishing here, dusting there
Cymbidium Faery works everywhere
Minding all the orchids' flowers
Gently tending all of them for hours

Dressed just like our orchids are
Full-petalled skirt like a pendulous star
This faery is so diligent
So many hours in toil are spent

Glossy leaves she lovingly
Polishes and shines with happy glee
For hours and hours without a rest
These glorious flowers are the best

For years on the end these orchids flower
Cymbidium Faery
Works for many an hour
Every day I thank her for her task
'Thank you and please never leave!'
Is all I ask

Cymbidium Faery

Gently tending all of them for hours • Polishing here, dusting there • Cymbidium Faery nooks everywhere • Minding all the orchids' flowers

Faeries West Kennet Long Barrow

Between this ancient mystical site
West Kennet Long Barrow
And that of the enigmatic Silbury Hill
There is a stream with water shallow
'Twas there I had an awesome thrill
A magical vision – What a sight!

What joy it was to hear the sounds
I hurried forth to see that in the water and all around
Were hundreds of tiny faeries flying and swimming
The water so clear and fast flowing
I stopped to take a look as faeries swam under the bridge
While others fluttered with their happy sound

Water Faeries dancing, laughing, and swimming
On a glorious summer's day
Flower Faeries them a-joining
In their happy play
As down we walked I was blessed to hear the sounds I knew
Faeries' laughter ringing out like tinkling bells anew

Faeries West Kennet Long Barrow

Water Faeries dancing, laughing, and swimming On a glorious summer's day Flower Faeries them a-joining In their happy play

Holly Grove

Surrounded by rectangular stone wall
Stones placed so beautifully
Row upon row horizontally
Then topped with more at ninety degrees

The cove of massive monoliths stands
Three lean inwards, their heads together
Seems like they've been like this forever

Around these stones, within the fence
Is such a potent ancient site
For there something not often seen
A Holly Grove

Holly is the ruler of the white realm, the winter
King of the dark half of the year
When all else is dormant, the Holly works hardest
Brightly verdant against the white landscape

Holly leaves are very prickly,
They are a metaphor
For protection, vigilance and stubborn victories won

Druids said that Holly trees repel lightning
Scientists now agree with this and more
Its distinctive leaf shape is naturally repelling
Holly's protective significance is more than just lore

Let your beauty shine even in times of dormancy
The energy of life is ever present
Messages from the holly tree
Whose colour shines, a lucky tree and, oh, so pleasant

So this ancient mystical Holly Grove
Gives protection to this sacred site
For those who come here when they rove
Will always treat it right

Holly Grove

An ancient Holly Grove • Around these stones, within the fence Is such a potent mystical site For there's something not often seen

Wellow Faeries

Just up the little road in Wellow
And over the pack-horse bridge
There's a lovely little stream that's rather shallow
But flowing quite briskly

The water seems to bounce and sing
It's clear and sweet and health giving
It rolls on down to meet the river
This one is truly a life-giver

To have a source of water so pure
Would help us many diseases to endure
The Devic Kingdom of this is aware
This is a secret they happily share

The Faery Folk who tend this stream
Make every drop of water gleam
Their magic here is no surprise
The little stream glistens before your eyes

So if ever you happen to visit Wellow
Do remember when you go
To sip mindfully of this sweet little stream
And be grateful, the Faery Folk will really beam

Wellow Faeries

So if you visit Wellow Do remember when you go To sip mindfully of this sweet little stream And be grateful, the Faery Folk will really beam •

Giant Bamboo Kalamunda

There he was all of two
Adventuring what he wished to do
Down the yard, up to the fence
Checking out the circumference

Giant Bamboo beckoned him
To explore what was within
Long rustling leaves and creaking uprights
Sliding over each other out of his sight

Dear two year old felt no fear
Seemed often to be drawn down here
Of dangers imminent I'd explain
But his fascination was so plain

No fear of snake within
Not even of death adders
Giant Bamboo home for this'n
Kingfishers, rats, frogs and others

Giant Bamboo screamed and yelled
As the wind blew through Whistle Pipe Gully
For the little lad to explore here
Would be quite a folly

Giant Bamboo called each day
But as he grew he learned to stay
In his garden and to play
But still admire and listen

Giant Bamboo Kalamunda

Sliding over each other out of his sight • Giant Bamboo beckoned him To explore what was within Long rustling leaves and creaking uprights

Blue Delphinium Faeries

Through verdant ivy clad stone arch
Enter the ancient walled garden
Standing upright in heavenly radiant blues
Lilac centred, dazzling azure hues
Are the glorious delphinium

Surrounded by faeries all abuzz
Working in beautiful harmony, not like us!
Each flower radiant to behold
Stalks so tall, indeed bold
Stories of their creation told

Bell-shaped lazuline flowers a'ringing
Faery Folk a'singing
They look, they laugh, then inquire
'Can you hear this sound we're a'bringing
This special shade of sapphire?'

'This flower's juice we use as ink
We mix with alum and in a blink
Our words we write as we think'
This flower is for the dolphin named
It nectary so shaped it is claimed

Communication through thought and word
Delphinium flowers can be heard
Calling to unusual species them to pollinate
Butterfly and bumble bee will joyfully congregate
Of the sweet, delicious nectar to partake

Blue Delphinium Faeries

Of the sweet, delicious nectar to partake • Calling to unusual species them to pollinate
Butterfly and bumble bee joyfully congregate

Holy Well St Barbe

Travel through St Barbe, this tiny town
Then in village turn in direction sinister
Follow tiny road then look through gap in trees
In direction sinister

For there is a well of stunning beauty
With healing pool in curved stone wall below
Rebuilt most carefully in all its old splendour
An aide to all who know

Water pure and sweet to taste
Fast flowing, so clear and clean
Sparkling, living, bubbling bright
This is certainly a healing site

All around the well is growing
A rose, climbing with unusual grace
Certainly not the kind of thing
To expect in this wintry place

Well, this is the most fabulous rose
For on it were yellow flowers
Buds and many an open one
All brilliant like the sun

Although this was the Yule Tide
In the month of December
When all around was icy cold
As one would remember

This tiny oasis of a spring
Actually maintained the vernal season
Best time for healing to bring
And the Faery Folk were the reason

Holy Well St Barbe

This is surely a healing site • Water pure and sweet to taste • Fast flowing, so clear and clean • Sparkling, living bubbling bright

Pine Tree near Hotié de Viviane

To find the Hotié de Viviane
In the Forêt de Brocéliande
Twas December when it we sought
And bitterly cold weather we fought

We walked along stony track at a pace
Seeking for signs of this ancient place
Looking here, looking there
No sign could we find anywhere

At last in angst I thought 'Is there anyone
Who can show us the Hotié de Viviane?'
To my right a huge pine tree shaking
Such a noise, like mighty wind, it was making

I stood at edge of leaf line and waited
The roaring sound had not abated
Under the tree I carefully walked
Then to my surprise the tree then talked

'Walk forward and you'll see a sign'
I felt a chill go up my spine
Together we walked following this advice
What a shock beheld our eyes

For past the pine upon the ground
A broken notice had we found
The place of the Queen of Faeries – Oh perfection!
Twas off in that very direction

So off to Hotié de Viviane we went
A feeling of awe, yet quite content
Pearls of mistletoe glistening on the stone
The Queen's monument standing all alone

Eventually we strolled back to the pine tree
And I thanked it Oh so joyfully
It was now still and quiet like all around
A little cone dropped on the ground
At my feet with nary a sound – A gift of memory

Pine Tree near Hotié de Viviane

What a shock beheld our eyes • 'Walk forward & you'll see a sign' I felt a chill up my spine. Together we walked following this advice

Forest Around Castel Franc

Castel Franc is such a potent site
At the Rock in front many ley lines
Cross both left and right
To lie on the Rock on a clear summer's night
The heavens above become a magical sight

For all is so active, clear and bright
Stars are shooting – Oh, what a sight!
The night sky is so crowded, it is such a shock
When one is lying on top of the Rock

By daylight to wander away from the Rock
The wildflowers with brilliant rainbow hues shine
Vibrant colours clear, glistening with morning dew
Are beckoning, calling to you

The orchids so fragile in violets and blue
In oranges and yellows of so many hues
The petals all shining, the leaves are too
Are beckoning, calling to you

Wild strawberries of delicate flavour abound
But please pick only one for it has been found
Though delicious and easily found on the ground
These wild fruits are there for the faeries

Yes, these fruits of the forest are for the faeries
They will share just a little if you ask them politely
They are awfully fond of this heart-shaped fruit
Wild strawberries, so tiny, tasty and cute

All around Castel Franc the forest can be seen
Growing so thickly, brambly and darkest green
But at the edges, just near the Rock
Live the Faery Folk, mostly unseen

Forest Around Castel Franc

When one is lying atop the Rock • Active, clear and bright Stars are shooting Oh what a sight! The night sky is so crowded, it is such a shock

Vortex Castel Franc

With Castel Franc at your back
Walk past the Chapel towards the track
Then where it bends off to the left
Something may happen, it seems quite daft

Stories of this spot abound
Where in it a small dog can become a huge hound
A little stripey domestic cat
Can appear ever so much bigger than that

For a child to walk into this spot
A giant stands but it is not
As this vicinity appears to be
A place of altered reality

For those who have the ability
A different kind of way to see
There is a vortex spinning here
That alters how things might appear

It is quite magical to stay a while
And watch what enters this tiny space
Such mystery to watch and see
For whatever goes into the spot
Becomes a mystery

Vortex Castel Franc

With Castel Franc at your back. Walk past the Chapel towards the track. Then where it bends off to the left. Something may happen, it seems quite daft.

Sainte Julianne

Over the meadow up the green grassy hill
Through the aged hobbit lands
Where folks used to live below the ground
In homes that are no longer sound

Past parasol pine tree to left of house
These pines were a subtle way of showing
That there is a place of sanctuary within
For those called heretics

At top of hill such a sacred site
Sainte Julianne - Goddess of the Light
Nine Sarcophagi in ruined Chapel lay
All feminine, one for Beatrice of Beziers

Halfway along the Chapel
A place of mystery
For the magic performed by the Smithy
His work with metal, wood, water and fire
Making what others could only aspire

Below the Chapel a Holy Well
Stillness where the water flows
Has refreshed many a pilgrim
Who to this ancient place goes

Then, Oh my, ten concave bowls
Carved into the Earth's rocky surface
Each deep enough to hold a man
One wonders of what their purpose

Seven wide steps lead up to the bowls
Other side of the Chapel
Young forest grows below these steps

To visit Sainte Julianne
On Mid-Summer's Eve
As full moon is a-rising
And watch the ancient procession gathering
To this feminine site they cleave

Tis indeed a place of initiation
The stone bowls ring out with sound
Creating wonderful harmonious vibrations
That brings beautiful sound all around

Sainte Julianne

All feminine, one Beatrice of Beziers • At top of hill a sacred site Sainte Julianne Goddess of the Light Nine Sarcophagi in ruined Chapel lay

La Magdalene Yoni Stone

Through small gate and stroll through herb garden
Up steps to the Templar House
A place of protection for this sacred and ancient
Feminine site of ours

Then turn, in your own time
And walk silently, alert, yet inwardly quiet
Just past small straggly tree
To the left one finds a magical place to be

Be still and honour, this very special
For in the wall on front of you
Is a perfect Yoni Stone

This perfectly shaped feminine form
By the Mother Earth
And running water born

Is indeed a place to stop and contemplate
The gentle energy bids you to wait
For some who stop at this knowledge gate
Have been blessed to have an epiphany

For those Keepers of this Ancient Site
Of the Mary Magdalene
Keep the knowledge for those with the right
To come here seeking understanding

La Magdalene Yoni Stone

La Magdalelene Ancient Cave

Deep in my dreams I often escape
To a cave with an egg-shaped window
In this place I sit with twelve more
Women in a circle the centre facing
One massive blue crystal at the core
Radiant, inner light glowing
Focus of our attention

Energy flows through us all
To this rock of beauteous perfection
Its auric field shimmers and expands
Then stunningly potent energy is emitted

Young ones placed around the circle
Watchful, ready to meet our physical needs
Mindful that in time they will
Take their place and do this deed

This cave of dreams is a reality
For I tell you now so truthfully
When I came upon this wondrous place
It really caused my heart to race
For part of me, the doubting side
Thought it was purely a dream site.

La Magdalene Ancient Cave

Stunningly potent energy is emitted • Energy flows through us all • To this rock of beauteous perfection • Its auric field shimmers and expands

Well South of St Barbe

Head south of St Barbe
Leave the aged church behind you
Turn right down a path
What a gorgeous site greets you

For we visited on a winter's day
In late December, and it was freezing
And though all about was icy
This area was alive, vibrant and like Spring

Here was a rectangular healing pool
Skilfully made from local stone
Filled with fresh and beautiful water cool
Flowing from a spring above

Beside this pool on the south corner
Were growing Shasta daisies
Deepest emerald green leaves and stalks adorn
And covered with so many flowers

The Shasta daisy flowers were opened wide
Perfect circles of petals, purest white
With sun-like centres of brilliant yellow
A Fibonacci spiral perfectly made

The Faery Folk were gathered here,
Working in a ring
And due to the wonder felt by humans
Are able to hold this wonderful healing place
Continually in the season of Spring

Well South of St Barbe

For we visited on a winter's day • In late December, and it was freezing • And though all about was icy • This area was alive, vibrant and like Spring

River Gum

Snowy white trunk with gentle hues of pink
Long flowing grey green leaves sweeping the ground
River Gum stands by the end of the cul-de-sac
Fine branches trailing to the ground

She loves the breeze that flows each day
Up through Whistle Pipe Gully
Her leaves dance with it so gently
Near the top of the valley

Her head is high, she grew so fast
But her branches all flow down
She moves Oh, so gracefully
Sweeping leaves along the ground

Normally this one would grow by a river
But in her home in Kalamunda
There's been no river – ever
To live on a hill above a town it truly is a wonder

She's peaceful here for beneath her roots
Flows a wondrous clear, clean spring
For her it meets so many needs
And good health does it bring

River Gum enjoys the sun shining upon her head
Knowing that every day the breeze will cool her down
To stand near her trunk, up close to her
And hear her speak, soft and clear

She talks about rivers under the Earth
That gave her breed of tree birth
Of winds and rains and sunny days
She really knows more than a penny's worth

River Gum

Near the top of the valley • She loves the breeze that flows each day Up through Whistle Pipe Gully Her leaves dance with it so gently

Violet Faeries

Violets have such delicate fragrance
Exquisite, unique, pure and sweet
Their flowers grow close to the earth
So neat, lovely and petite

The hues of violet are so lovely
Delicate lilacs to deepest purples
Touches of brightest yellow within
Five petalled glory

To sit beside the violet patch
As a child my heart would catch
For so many Violet Faeries lived there
The sweet little violets drew me near

The violet leaves deepest emerald green
Created shelters and were kept so clean
Other folk would rush right by
Like there was nothing to be seen

But I'd visit there most every day
And with the Violet Faeries I would stay
To watch, laugh, play and learn
Later on to be with them I'd yearn

We could talk about mankind
Though I'd not speak aloud
They'd seem to listen to my mind
In this strange world they were always kind

For Violet Faeries love the Earth
This is why they live so near
If you should happen upon a violet patch
Watch for them, for they will be here

Violet Faeries

Five petalled glory • The hues of violet are so lovely • Delicate lilacs to deepest purples • Touches of brightest yellow within

Water Faeries – Mount Pleasant

Down to the river as a child I went
So many hours down there I spent
Playing in the reeds, the trees, the water
Perhaps more time than I ought'a!

One day an ancient Paper Bark Tree whispered to me
And said to climb up on a branch to see
I obeyed so readily
Up, Up I climbed so gleefully
And lay face down along a branch

This limb the river overhang
From below strange voices rang
I looked below and to my surprise
Water Faeries were playing before my eyes

They laughed and tinkled and danced and swam
Flipped into the water
And onto the land

The joy was infectious
My smile radiant
The water shone golden and clear and clean
It was a most wondrous sight to have seen

My gratitude to the lovely tree
For opening this world to me
Was immense as I lay along his branch
To leave this place was such a wrench

For years I went back to the Paper Bark Tree
That had taught Oh, so thoughtfully
And watched the Water Faeries
Play together happily

Water Faeries – Mount Pleasant

They laughed and tinkled and danced and swam and dipped into the water and onto the land. The joy was infectious.

Indian Coral Tree

At the very end of the cul-de-sac
The Indian Coral Tree stood near the track
This one was very old, its trunk so worn

The base of its trunk felt sharp and rough
To climb this tree was awfully tough
For all younger branches were covered in thorns

The Indian Coral Tree was covered with life
Birds and insects had no strife
Living on its glorious scarlet red flowers

One summer day to my surprise
Two young lads ran inside with cries
'The Tree's screaming, Mum! Come quick!'

The boys were right
Their words were true
I heard her screams loud and true

As we stood and watched helplessly
A massive branch twisted round and round
And threw itself upon the ground

We stood there in great surprise
Wiping tears of shock from our eyes
The tree had screamed in such pain

A drought is such a tragic experience
To the Indian Coral tree it was plain
We never wanted it to have that stress again

Indian Coral Tree

The Indian Coral Tree was covered with life. Birds and insects had no strife. Living on its glorious scarlet red flowers.

Tingle Forest

Compose yourself
For this experience
Be still – prepare yourself
This is unique
You are to enter
The Valley of the Giants

Enter the silence
Amongst the Giants
Huge eyes watch you walk slowly by
Massive Tree Devas thee espy
'How can I help thee?' I cry
'Awe, Respect, Honour' The reply

Beneath their mighty trunks one stands
Unique experience in southern lands
Silence
Silence
How grand it is to understand reality

Tingle Forest

How grand it is to understand reality • Beneath their mighty trunks one stands Unique experience in southern lands Silence Silence

Grandma Tingle

Slowly walk along meandering path
Through the Valley of the Ancients
Suddenly an enormous tree – Oh, laugh!
It is Grandma Tingle

Her nose one sees in profile
A wondrous shape indeed
Upon her trunk bulging eyes too
Some run past her at speed!

'Oh she's watching me!' you think
As you approach and then go past
Her eyes are open, nary a blink
This feeling may well last

Have a plan and take a pace
Then turn around and watch her face
Is it your imagination
Or is she going in your direction?

Then set off again along the way
And listen to the silence this day
When again you turn – Has she moved?
Grandma Tingle? Can it be proved?

But some folk feel that as past they go
This statuesque giant moves but ever so slow!
Slowly, slowly, but have no fears
She's been moving now for four hundred years!

Grandma Tingle

Her nose one sees in profile • A wondrous shape indeed • Upon her trunk bulging eyes too • Some run past her at speed

Snowy Mountain Gum

'Twas the summer when we climbed Mount Kosciusko
So lovely in the Snowy Mountain Range
Beside the path were trees Oh, so strange
The Snowy Mountain Gum

As we walked along the way to Kosciusko
These trees were gathered along each side
Making the most incredible shapes you know
I wondered what they could hide

Their branches and roots seemed to become as one
All twisted and twined together
Rainbow colours of light in their bark
Whirling and shining forever

Snowy Mountain Gums felt ageless
A total joy to behold
For a moment I thought they were faceless
Just all gnarled and so very old

Then I stopped and stood quietly
Allowing all others to pass by me
Then low and behold what did I see?
A stunningly ancient Tree Deva watching me

What a mystical gift was this?
I stood and stared, I bowed in greeting
And realised the trunks and branches and roots
Were all part of this wonderful wise being

Snowy Mountain Gum

Snowy Mountain Gums felt ageless • At total joy to behold • For a moment I thought they were faceless • Just all gnarled and so very old

Wattle Faeries

Expressing the radiance of the mighty sun
Winter flowering when many other trees rest
Glorious yellows to that I'll attest
Tended by the Wattle Faeries, every one

Fluttering happily
In and around the tiny puffy balls of brilliant yellows
Working industriously
These bright little fellows

Hardy seeds need heat, even fire
To burst and then germinate
So after bush fire devastation entire
The wattle will always propagate

Fluffy orbs so dazzling and sunny
Emit a fragrant yet heady perfume
Your senses do consume
Globular balls of sunlit honey

Busy bees work these glorious trees
The nectar in very fine pollen
Low sucrose, high fructose honey clear and pure
Delicious and healthy

The Faery Folk who tend the Wattle
Know they have many uses for mankind
Branches for wattle and daub, bark in tanning
Blossoms in perfume making

Wattle Faeries tend this tree
Which works so hard when others rest
Meeting the needs of man, bird and bee
Brilliant sun-like yellows, truly the best

Wattle Faeries

Fluffy orbs so dazzling and sunny · Emit a fragrant yet heady perfume · Your senses do consume · Globular balls of sunlit honey · Busy bees work these glorious trees ·

Silk Cotton Tree

Growing majestically
Stretching towards the heavens
Smooth grey white trunks reaching ever upwards

Thorn ridged, mighty flying buttresses
Encircle the base and
Support the massive trunk
Inspiration for the architects
Of castles and cathedrals
The engineers of bridges and viaducts

Canopy of deepest green leaves atop
Creating shade for all that grows below.
Silk Cotton Tree is king of the jungle
Enormous, erect and regal

Regarding all below from on high
Winds whispering through with a sigh
Home for insect, birds and vines
With their weight your trunk will not incline

Oh wisdom keeper as a tree
Overseeing the forest naturally
Protector of all who live upon and below
Observing from above
In jungle or beside river all a flow
Oh so much do you know

Growing majestically
Skywards and earthwards ever growing
As above so below
You are knowing

Silk Cotton Tree

As Above So Below • Growing majestically Stretching towards the heavens Smooth grey white trunks reaching ever upwards

The Poplar Tree

Elegant, conicular giant tree
Growing around the perimeter of the property
Sixty feet high or even more
So many of them, at least a score

Shaped like a rocket
Conicular perfection
Branches stretched upwards in vertical direction

One such tree, so magnetic
For climbing, so tempting
Called to the small child
For him to come climbing

This child was intrigued
And heeded this call
He whizzed right up to the top
With never a thought that he could fall

From below it looked like
He was on a great ship
At the top of a massive mast
Perhaps he'd lived this in his lives past

The Poplar Tree

Called to the small child For him to come climbing This child was intrigued And heeded this call He whizzed right up to the top With never a thought that he could fall

Our Faraway Tree

Once we read 'The Faraway Tree'
A book about fairies
All about a tall gum tree
Like this one exactly

If we creep up to its base
And on it place our little face
Then call softly, kindly, sweetly
And be still and listen
For if we do this correctly
The fairies will come

So up we go respectfully
To the massive base of the gum tree
And on the rough, lichen covered bark place our face
Then we call softly, kindly, sweetly
And be still and listen
The fairies do come
For in our back garden we have indeed
Our own Faraway Tree

With thanks to Enid Blyton!

Our Faraway Tree

If we creep up to its base   And on it place our little face   Then call softly, kindly, sweetly   And be still and listen for the fairies will come

Holly's Faery Garden

'Come down the garden behind the big shed
You'll find them there' young Holly said
Past the pizza oven, wheelbarrow, rake
Is Holly's garden yet awake?

My hand she grasped as down we stepped
To Holly's Faery Garden
In her sweet hand dear Holly grasped
Two porcelain faeries just given

She gathered all her faeries and placed in the hollow tree
'Will you welcome Silver and Moon?'
She left them in conference: one, two, so many
Positive decision made quite soon

Suddenly it came to me
This place is quite a flutter
With tinkling laughter and filled with glee
So many faeries came that day
To play in Holly's Fairy Garden

Holly's Faery Garden

My hand she grasped as down we stepped To Holly's Faery Garden In her sweet hand bear Holly grasped Two porcelain faeries just given

Camphor Laurel Tree

Leaves that bud from softest rose pink
And become the brightest green I think
Roots spread out atop the soil
This magnificent giant does surely toil

Over her feet deepest shades of green ivy
And around her trunk wisteria and ivy entwining
To flow in wondrous perfumed lilac glory
And mark the start of Spring

In days of heat when wind was light
Her arm held out, sheltered from the bright
My babies rested in that gentle sully
Of the breeze that came up Whistle Pipe Gully

As years went by I found it great
To sit on her arm and meditate
As upon her branch I rested
The Camphor Laurel I surely tested

'With crystal clear springs that surface here
A stone circle I feel could be placed so near
If you would please give me a sign
Of where should be this circle so fine'

She answered me with a shudder
Her branches began to whirl
In front of me in the air
Was created a vortex whirlpool
The ground was cleared of leaf and litter

In front of me at my very feet
A perfect circle, oh so neat
The Camphor Laurel had created

The stones then came from near and far
Some were collected in my car
I rolled them down the property
And made a pile beside this tree

Rose quartz, amethyst,
Picture jasper and mookaite
How to place them was my plight
These stones were heavy and I'm not so strong
To put them in place would not be right

So down upon the branch I sat
And I asked 'How can I do that?
The stones are here but not in a ring
Please help me to do this thing.'
'Close your eyes and trust'
Was her reply,
'You'll lift them all by and by'

So I did as instructed.
Eyes shut tight and trusted
Put out my hands and lifted the first
Turned and placed in under the tree
Then did this action repeatedly
Until the stones twenty two
Formed a circle of nine feet

Created a serene and healing sanctuary
Underneath her shady branches
Her spinning vortex always
Kept the circle clean of leaves

Camphor Laurel Tree

In front of me at my very feet At perfect circle oh so neat The Camphor Laurel had created The stones then came from near & far •

Acknowledgements

Firstly my sincere gratitude goes to my lovely mother, Mary Mell, who gave me the freedom as a child to explore the bush and river near to our Western Australian home. Through her love of gardening I was blessed to learn to appreciate and study the plant kingdom.

Also my appreciation goes to my dear late husband Keith Harken and our wonderful children Russell, Steele, Brietta and Tiffany, and daughters-in-law Kristy and Julie. We have so many happy memories of time spent together in the bush, rivers and oceans. They have always given great encouragement to my endeavours.

My gratitude goes to my husband, Mervyn Smith, for the many exciting hours we have spent together dowsing and investigating ancient mystical and fairy sites. Without Mervyn's encouragement this book may not have been written. Through his amazing ability with graphic design he has helped to create this beautiful art form.

I give my heartfelt thankfulness always to the Devic Realms and the Faery Kingdoms for the inspirational insights and the wisdom they have chosen to share with me, from early childhood to the present day. Through these understandings I too have gained a degree of wisdom and awareness of the tasks that these ones undertake on our behalf.

Finally, but most importantly, I give great gratitude to the Mother Earth for providing a space refuge for humanity where we can learn to work with the Devic Kingdom in a positive and co-operative manner.

About the Author

Joy Lynette Smith hails from Western Australia and was born in Mount Pleasant, a beautiful Perth suburb, near the river and surrounded by bush. It was there she first discovered the Devic Realms through fairies, trees and flowers.

She developed an intuitive sensitivity and clairvoyance from an early age. During her childhood she spent many hours in the Australian bush, by rivers and the Indian Ocean and developed a deep love and awareness of nature and a growing sense of awareness of the energies inherent in the environment.

With her late husband Keith Harken and their four children she lived on the outskirts of the city in Kalamunda on a huge property, surrounded by massive trees, right on the edge of the escarpment and the bush.

Joy has broadened her parameters through experiencing the miraculous gift of being healed many years after her spine was fractured whilst going through a car windscreen. This has left her in awe of the amazing healing that is possible and given her renewed energy and direction. Joy is an exceptional healer.

Since 2005 she has held fascinating retreats, especially in the English Lake District, where she has helped to introduce people to the Faery Folk and Devic Realms.

She now lives in London with her husband, Mervyn. She has visited many ancient and devic sites on our beautiful planet and shares some of her experiences in this book.

Edwards Brothers Malloy
Thorofare, NJ USA
March 8, 2013